THIS CRUISE JOURNAL BELONGS TO:

CRUISE SAVINGS

WE'RE SAVING FOR: _____

AMOUNT NEEDED: _____

OUR GOAL DATE: [   ]

$

DEPOSIT TRACKER

AMOUNT DEPOSITED:	DATE DEPOSITED:
$	
$	
$	
$	
$	
$	
$	
$	
$	
$	

CRUISE SAVINGS

DEPOSIT TRACKER

AMOUNT DEPOSITED: DATE DEPOSITED:

$ _____   _____

$ _____   _____

$ _____   _____

$ _____   _____

$ _____   _____

$ _____   _____

$ _____   _____

$ _____   _____

$ _____   _____

$ _____   _____

$ _____   _____

$ _____   _____

$ _____   _____

CRUISE DETAILS

NOTES

TO DO:

CRUISE DETAILS & REMINDERS:

FLIGHT INFORMATION

DATE: _____ DESTINATION: _____

AIRLINE:	
BOOKING NUMBER:	
DEPARTURE DATE:	
BOARDING TIME:	
GATE NUMBER	
SEAT NUMBER:	
ARRIVAL / LANDING TIME:	

DATE: _____ DESTINATION: _____

AIRLINE:	
BOOKING NUMBER:	
DEPARTURE DATE:	
BOARDING TIME:	
GATE NUMBER:	
SEAT NUMBER:	
ARRIVAL / LANDING TIME:	

FLIGHT INFORMATION

DATE:	DESTINATION:

AIRLINE:	
BOOKING NUMBER:	
DEPARTURE DATE:	
BOARDING TIME:	
GATE NUMBER:	
SEAT NUMBER:	
ARRIVAL / LANDING TIME:	

DATE:	DESTINATION:

AIRLINE:	
BOOKING NUMBER:	
DEPARTURE DATE:	
BOARDING TIME:	
GATE NUMBER:	
SEAT NUMBER:	
ARRIVAL / LANDING TIME:	

TRAIN INFORMATION

DATE:	DESTINATION:

DEPARTING STATION:	
TICKET TYPE:	
DEPARTURE DATE:	
BOARDING TIME:	
GATE NUMBER	
SEAT NUMBER:	
ARRIVAL / LANDING TIME:	

DATE:	DESTINATION:

AIRLINE:	
BOOKING NUMBER:	
DEPARTURE DATE:	
BOARDING TIME:	
GATE NUMBER:	
SEAT NUMBER:	
ARRIVAL / LANDING TIME:	

CAR INFORMATION

DATE: PICK-UP LOCATION:

CAR RENTAL COMPANY:	
VEHICLE TYPE:	
DEPARTURE DATE:	
PICK-UP TIME:	
INSPECTION NOTES:	
COST PER DAY:	
RETURN DATE:	

DATE: PICK-UP LOCATION::

CAR RENTAL COMPANY:	
VEHICLE TYPE:	
DEPARTURE DATE:	
PICK-UP TIME:	
INSPECTION NOTES:	
COST PER DAY:	
RETURN DATE:	

PACKING CHECKLIST

CLOTHING FOR HER	✓	CLOTHING FOR HIM	✓

ESSENTIALS	✓	FOR THE JOURNEY	✓
		IMPORTANT DOCUMENTS	✓

CRUISE PACKING CHECKLIST

CLOTHING	✓	ESSENTIALS	✓

CRUISE EXCURSION PLANNER

ACTIVITY / EXCURSION OVERVIEW:

EST COST OF EXCURSION: _____

INCLUSIONS:	✓		**EXCLUSIONS:**	✓
FOOD & DRINK:	☐		_____	☐
TRANSPORTATION:	☐		_____	☐
GRATUITY:	☐		_____	☐

ACTUAL COST: [   ]

IMPORTANT INFORMATION:

CONTACT: _____   PHONE #: _____

MEET UP TIME: _____   WHAT TO BRING: _____

ADDRESS: _____

CRUISE EXCURSION PLANNER

ACTIVITY / EXCURSION OVERVIEW:

EST COST OF EXCURSION:

INCLUSIONS:	✓	**EXCLUSIONS:**	✓
FOOD & DRINK:	☐		☐
TRANSPORTATION:	☐		☐
GRATUITY:	☐		☐

ACTUAL COST:

IMPORTANT INFORMATION:

CONTACT: _____ PHONE #: _____

MEET UP TIME: _____ WHAT TO BRING: _____

ADDRESS: _____

CRUISE EXCURSION PLANNER

ACTIVITY / EXCURSION OVERVIEW:

EST COST OF EXCURSION:

INCLUSIONS:	✓	**EXCLUSIONS:**	✓
FOOD & DRINK:	☐		☐
TRANSPORTATION:	☐		☐
GRATUITY:	☐		☐

ACTUAL COST:

IMPORTANT INFORMATION:

CONTACT: _____   PHONE #: _____

MEET UP TIME: _____   WHAT TO BRING: _____

ADDRESS: _____

CRUISE EXCURSION PLANNER

ACTIVITY / EXCURSION OVERVIEW:

EST COST OF EXCURSION:

INCLUSIONS:	✓	**EXCLUSIONS:**	✓
FOOD & DRINK:	☐		☐
TRANSPORTATION:	☐		☐
GRATUITY:	☐		☐

ACTUAL COST:

IMPORTANT INFORMATION:

CONTACT: _____   PHONE #: _____

MEET UP TIME: _____   WHAT TO BRING: _____

ADDRESS: _____

CRUISE PORT PLANNER

DESTINATION: **DATE:**

THINGS TO DO / SEE:

WHERE TO EAT:

TRANSPORTATION DETAILS:

OTHER INFORMATION:

RETURN TO SHIP BY:

CRUISE PORT PLANNER

DESTINATION: DATE:

THINGS TO DO / SEE:

WHERE TO EAT:

TRANSPORTATION DETAILS:

OTHER INFORMATION:

RETURN TO SHIP BY:

CRUISE PORT PLANNER

DESTINATION: DATE:

THINGS TO DO / SEE:

☐
☐
☐
☐
☐
☐
☐

WHERE TO EAT:

☐
☐
☐
☐
☐
☐
☐

TRANSPORTATION DETAILS:

☐
☐
☐
☐
☐

OTHER INFORMATION:

☐
☐
☐
☐
☐

RETURN TO SHIP BY:

CRUISE PORT PLANNER

DESTINATION:	DATE:

THINGS TO DO / SEE:

WHERE TO EAT:

TRANSPORTATION DETAILS:

OTHER INFORMATION:

RETURN TO SHIP BY:

CRUISE PORT PLANNER

DESTINATION:	DATE:

THINGS TO DO / SEE:

WHERE TO EAT:

TRANSPORTATION DETAILS:

OTHER INFORMATION:

RETURN TO SHIP BY:

CRUISE PORT PLANNER

DESTINATION:	DATE:

THINGS TO DO / SEE:

WHERE TO EAT:

TRANSPORTATION DETAILS:

OTHER INFORMATION:

RETURN TO SHIP BY:

CRUISE PORT PLANNER

DESTINATION: DATE:

THINGS TO DO / SEE:

WHERE TO EAT:

TRANSPORTATION DETAILS:

OTHER INFORMATION:

RETURN TO SHIP BY:

CRUISE PORT PLANNER

DESTINATION: DATE:

THINGS TO DO / SEE:

WHERE TO EAT:

TRANSPORTATION DETAILS:

OTHER INFORMATION:

RETURN TO SHIP BY:

CRUISE PORT PLANNER

DESTINATION: DATE:

THINGS TO DO / SEE:

WHERE TO EAT:

TRANSPORTATION DETAILS:

OTHER INFORMATION:

RETURN TO SHIP BY:

CRUISE PORT PLANNER

DESTINATION:	DATE:

THINGS TO DO / SEE:

- [ ]
- [ ]
- [ ]
- [ ]
- [ ]
- [ ]
- [ ]

WHERE TO EAT:

- [ ]
- [ ]
- [ ]
- [ ]
- [ ]
- [ ]
- [ ]

TRANSPORTATION DETAILS:

- [ ]
- [ ]
- [ ]
- [ ]
- [ ]

OTHER INFORMATION:

- [ ]
- [ ]
- [ ]
- [ ]
- [ ]

RETURN TO SHIP BY:

CRUISE PORT PLANNER

DESTINATION:	DATE:

THINGS TO DO / SEE:

WHERE TO EAT:

TRANSPORTATION DETAILS:

OTHER INFORMATION:

RETURN TO SHIP BY:

CRUISE PORT PLANNER

DESTINATION:	DATE:

THINGS TO DO / SEE:

☐
☐
☐
☐
☐
☐
☐

WHERE TO EAT:

☐
☐
☐
☐
☐
☐
☐

TRANSPORTATION DETAILS:

☐
☐
☐
☐
☐

OTHER INFORMATION:

☐
☐
☐
☐
☐

RETURN TO SHIP BY:

CRUISE PORT PLANNER

DESTINATION: DATE:

THINGS TO DO / SEE:

WHERE TO EAT:

TRANSPORTATION DETAILS:

OTHER INFORMATION:

RETURN TO SHIP BY:

CRUISE PORT PLANNER

DESTINATION: DATE:

THINGS TO DO / SEE:

☐
☐
☐
☐
☐
☐
☐

WHERE TO EAT:

☐
☐
☐
☐
☐
☐
☐

TRANSPORTATION DETAILS:

☐
☐
☐
☐
☐

OTHER INFORMATION:

☐
☐
☐
☐
☐

RETURN TO SHIP BY:

ALL ABOARD!

PRE-CRUISE TO DO LIST & CHECKLIST

1 MONTH BEFORE

2 WEEKS BEFORE

1 WEEK BEFORE

2 DAYS BEFORE

24 HOURS BEFORE

DAY OF TRAVEL

CRUISE PLANNER

WEEK OF:

MONDAY	TUESDAY	WEDNESDAY	THURSDAY
TO DO	TO DO	TO DO	TO DO
MEALS	MEALS	MEALS	MEALS

FRIDAY	SATURDAY	SUNDAY	NOTES
TO DO	TO DO	TO DO	
MEALS	MEALS	MEALS	MEALS

CRUISE PLANNER

WEEK OF:

MONDAY	TUESDAY	WEDNESDAY	THURSDAY
TO DO	TO DO	TO DO	TO DO
MEALS	MEALS	MEALS	MEALS

FRIDAY	SATURDAY	SUNDAY	NOTES
TO DO	TO DO	TO DO	
MEALS	MEALS	MEALS	MEALS

CRUISING TO DO LIST

CRUISE BUCKET LIST

PLACES I WANT TO VISIT:

THINGS I WANT TO SEE:

TOP 3 DESTINATIONS:

CRUISE ITINERARY

Monday

Tuesday

Wednesday

Thursday

Friday

Saturday

Sunday

CRUISE ITINERARY

Monday

Tuesday

Wednesday

Thursday

Friday

Saturday

Sunday

CRUISE ITINERARY

Monday

Tuesday

Wednesday

Thursday

Friday

Saturday

Sunday

CRUISE OVERVIEW

MONTH:

MONDAY	TUESDAY	WEDNESDAY	THURSDAY	FRIDAY	SATURDAY	SUNDAY

CRUISE ACTIVITIES

WEEKLY ACTIVITY TRACKER: **M   T   W   T   F   S   S**

DAILY ACTIVITY PLANNER

DAILY ITINERARY

ACTIVITY: _____

TIME: _____

LOCATION: _____

WEATHER: ☀️ ⛅ 🌦️ ☁️ ⛈️

MEAL PLANNER

DAILY EXPENSES

_____ _____

_____ _____

_____ _____

_____ _____

TOTAL COST: [   ]

TOP ACTIVITIES

TIME:	SCHEDULE:

NOTES:

DAILY ACTIVITY PLANNER

DAILY ITINERARY

ACTIVITY: _____

TIME: _____

LOCATION: _____

WEATHER: ☀ ⛅ 🌦 ☁ ⛈

MEAL PLANNER

DAILY EXPENSES

_____   _____

_____   _____

_____   _____

_____   _____

TOTAL COST: [_____]

TOP ACTIVITIES

TIME:	SCHEDULE:

NOTES:

DAILY ACTIVITY PLANNER

DAILY ITINERARY

ACTIVITY: _____

TIME: _____

LOCATION: _____

WEATHER: ☀ ⛅ 🌦 ☁ ⛈

MEAL PLANNER

DAILY EXPENSES

_____   _____

_____   _____

_____   _____

_____   _____

_____

TOTAL COST: [_____]

TOP ACTIVITIES

TIME:	SCHEDULE:

NOTES:

DAILY ACTIVITY PLANNER

DAILY ITINERARY

ACTIVITY: _____

TIME: _____

LOCATION: _____

WEATHER: ☀ ⛅ 🌦 ☁ ⛈

MEAL PLANNER

TOP ACTIVITIES

TIME: SCHEDULE:

DAILY EXPENSES

TOTAL COST: [_____]

NOTES:

DAILY ACTIVITY PLANNER

DAILY ITINERARY

ACTIVITY: _____

TIME: _____

LOCATION: _____

WEATHER: ☀ ⛅ 🌦 ☁ ⛈

MEAL PLANNER

DAILY EXPENSES

TOTAL COST: [ ]

TOP ACTIVITIES

TIME:	SCHEDULE:

NOTES:

DAILY ACTIVITY PLANNER

DAILY ITINERARY

ACTIVITY: _____

TIME: _____

LOCATION: _____

WEATHER: ☀ ⛅ 🌦 ☁ ⛈

MEAL PLANNER

DAILY EXPENSES

_____ _____

_____ _____

_____ _____

_____ _____

_____ _____

TOTAL COST: [   ]

TOP ACTIVITIES

TIME: SCHEDULE:

NOTES:

DAILY ACTIVITY PLANNER

DAILY ITINERARY

ACTIVITY: _____

TIME: _____

LOCATION: _____

WEATHER:

TOP ACTIVITIES

MEAL PLANNER

TIME: SCHEDULE:

DAILY EXPENSES

TOTAL COST:

NOTES:

DAILY ACTIVITY PLANNER

DAILY ITINERARY

ACTIVITY: _____

TIME: _____

LOCATION: _____

WEATHER: ☀️ ⛅ 🌦️ ☁️ ⛈️

MEAL PLANNER

DAILY EXPENSES

_____ _____

_____ _____

_____ _____

_____ _____

_____

TOTAL COST: [_____]

TOP ACTIVITIES

TIME:	SCHEDULE:

NOTES:

DAILY ACTIVITY PLANNER

DAILY ITINERARY

ACTIVITY: _____

TIME: _____

LOCATION: _____

WEATHER: ☀ ⛅ 🌦 ☁ ⛈

MEAL PLANNER

DAILY EXPENSES

TOTAL COST: [   ]

TOP ACTIVITIES

TIME: SCHEDULE:

NOTES:

DAILY ACTIVITY PLANNER

DAILY ITINERARY

ACTIVITY: _____

TIME: _____

LOCATION: _____

WEATHER:

MEAL PLANNER

TOP ACTIVITIES

TIME:	SCHEDULE:

DAILY EXPENSES

TOTAL COST: [   ]

NOTES:

CRUISE FRIENDS

FRIENDS ARE FOREVER

NAME:

PHONE NUMBER:

ADDRESS:

CABIN #:

FRIENDS ARE FOREVER

NAME:

PHONE NUMBER:

ADDRESS:

CABIN #:

FRIENDS ARE FOREVER

NAME:

PHONE NUMBER:

ADDRESS:

CABIN #:

FRIENDS ARE FOREVER

NAME:

PHONE NUMBER:

ADDRESS:

CABIN #:

There's Nothing Like Cruising Life!

CRUISE FRIENDS

FRIENDS ARE FOREVER

NAME:

PHONE NUMBER:

ADDRESS:

CABIN #:

FRIENDS ARE FOREVER

NAME:

PHONE NUMBER:

ADDRESS:

CABIN #:

FRIENDS ARE FOREVER

NAME:

PHONE NUMBER:

ADDRESS:

CABIN #:

FRIENDS ARE FOREVER

NAME:

PHONE NUMBER:

ADDRESS:

CABIN #:

There's Nothing Like Cruising Life!

CRUISE FRIENDS

FRIENDS ARE FOREVER

NAME:

PHONE NUMBER:

ADDRESS:

CABIN #:

FRIENDS ARE FOREVER

NAME:

PHONE NUMBER:

ADDRESS:

CABIN #:

FRIENDS ARE FOREVER

NAME:

PHONE NUMBER:

ADDRESS:

CABIN #:

FRIENDS ARE FOREVER

NAME:

PHONE NUMBER:

ADDRESS:

CABIN #:

There's Nothing Like Cruising Life!

CRUISE FRIENDS

FRIENDS ARE FOREVER

NAME:

PHONE NUMBER:

ADDRESS:

CABIN #:

FRIENDS ARE FOREVER

NAME:

PHONE NUMBER:

ADDRESS:

CABIN #:

FRIENDS ARE FOREVER

NAME:

PHONE NUMBER:

ADDRESS:

CABIN #:

FRIENDS ARE FOREVER

NAME:

PHONE NUMBER:

ADDRESS:

CABIN #:

There's Nothing Like Cruising Life!

MY CRUISE AGENDA

MY CRUISE JOURNAL

DATE:

What I Did Today:

Highlight of the Day:

Thoughts & Reflections:

MY CRUISE JOURNAL

DATE:

What I Did Today:

Highlight of the Day:

Thoughts & Reflections:

MY CRUISE JOURNAL

DATE:

What I Did Today:

Highlight of the Day:

Thoughts & Reflections:

MY CRUISE JOURNAL

DATE:

What I Did Today:

Highlight of the Day:

Thoughts & Reflections:

MY CRUISE JOURNAL

DATE:

What I Did Today:

Highlight of the Day:

Thoughts & Reflections:

MY CRUISE JOURNAL

DATE:

What I Did Today:

Highlight of the Day:

Thoughts & Reflections:

MY CRUISE JOURNAL

DATE:

What I Did Today:

Highlight of the Day:

Thoughts & Reflections:

MY CRUISE JOURNAL

DATE:

What I Did Today:

Highlight of the Day:

Thoughts & Reflections:

MY CRUISE JOURNAL

DATE:

What I Did Today:

Highlight of the Day:

Thoughts & Reflections:

MY CRUISE JOURNAL

DATE:

What I Did Today:

Highlight of the Day:

Thoughts & Reflections:

MY CRUISE JOURNAL

DATE:

What I Did Today:

Highlight of the Day:

Thoughts & Reflections:

MY CRUISE JOURNAL

DATE:

What I Did Today:

Highlight of the Day:

Thoughts & Reflections:

MY CRUISE JOURNAL

DATE:

What I Did Today:

Highlight of the Day:

Thoughts & Reflections:

MY CRUISE JOURNAL

DATE:

What I Did Today:

Highlight of the Day:

Thoughts & Reflections:

CRUISE SAVINGS

WE'RE SAVING FOR: _____

AMOUNT NEEDED: _____

OUR GOAL DATE: _____

$

DEPOSIT TRACKER

AMOUNT DEPOSITED:	DATE DEPOSITED:
$	
$	
$	
$	
$	
$	
$	
$	
$	
$	

CRUISE SAVINGS

DEPOSIT TRACKER

AMOUNT DEPOSITED: DATE DEPOSITED:

$

$

$

$

$

$

$

$

$

$

$

$

$

CRUISE DETAILS

NOTES

TO DO:

CRUISE DETAILS & REMINDERS:

FLIGHT INFORMATION

DATE:	DESTINATION:

AIRLINE:	
BOOKING NUMBER:	
DEPARTURE DATE:	
BOARDING TIME:	
GATE NUMBER	
SEAT NUMBER:	
ARRIVAL / LANDING TIME:	

DATE:	DESTINATION:

AIRLINE:	
BOOKING NUMBER:	
DEPARTURE DATE:	
BOARDING TIME:	
GATE NUMBER	
SEAT NUMBER:	
ARRIVAL / LANDING TIME:	

FLIGHT INFORMATION

DATE: _____   DESTINATION: _____

AIRLINE:	
BOOKING NUMBER:	
DEPARTURE DATE:	
BOARDING TIME:	
GATE NUMBER	
SEAT NUMBER:	
ARRIVAL / LANDING TIME:	

DATE: _____   DESTINATION: _____

AIRLINE:	
BOOKING NUMBER:	
DEPARTURE DATE:	
BOARDING TIME:	
GATE NUMBER:	
SEAT NUMBER:	
ARRIVAL / LANDING TIME:	

TRAIN INFORMATION

DATE:	DESTINATION:

DEPARTING STATION:	
TICKET TYPE:	
DEPARTURE DATE:	
BOARDING TIME:	
GATE NUMBER:	
SEAT NUMBER:	
ARRIVAL / LANDING TIME:	

DATE:	DESTINATION:

AIRLINE:	
BOOKING NUMBER:	
DEPARTURE DATE:	
BOARDING TIME:	
GATE NUMBER:	
SEAT NUMBER:	
ARRIVAL / LANDING TIME:	

CAR INFORMATION

DATE: _____   PICK-UP LOCATION: _____

CAR RENTAL COMPANY:	
VEHICLE TYPE:	
DEPARTURE DATE:	
PICK-UP TIME:	
INSPECTION NOTES:	
COST PER DAY:	
RETURN DATE:	

DATE: _____   PICK-UP LOCATION:: _____

CAR RENTAL COMPANY:	
VEHICLE TYPE:	
DEPARTURE DATE:	
PICK-UP TIME:	
INSPECTION NOTES:	
COST PER DAY:	
RETURN DATE:	

CRUISE COUNTDOWN

MONTH: _____   YEAR: _____

M	T	W	T	F	S	S

PACKING LIST IDEAS

CLOTHING FOR HER	✓	CLOTHING FOR HIM	✓
T-Shirts &, Tank Tops & Blouses		T-Shirts & Tank Tops	
Sundresses		Shorts	
Flip Flops, Sandals & Heels		Swim Wear	
Shorts & Pants		Jeans, Khakis	
Swimsuit & Cover Up		Formal Attire (dress shirt, shoes, etc.)	
Purses		Belt	
Aqua/Swimming Shoes		Tie	
Bras, Panties & Socks		Sandals / Sneakers	
Sunhat		Visor, Baseball Cap	
Sunglasses		Watch	
Formal Attire		Sunglasses	
Jewelry		Socks & Underwear	

ESSENTIALS	✓	FOR THE JOURNEY	✓
Sporting Goods		Carry On Bag	
Suntan Lotion		Cash / Local Currency	
Medication (motion sickness, etc.)		Credit Cards	
Travel Mug / Water Bottle		Phone Charger	
Games		Backpack	
Jacket		**IMPORTANT DOCUMENTS**	✓
Toiletries		Passport & ID	
Hiking Boots		Cruise Documents & Boarding Pass	
		Flight Information	

PACKING CHECKLIST

CLOTHING FOR HER	✓	CLOTHING FOR HIM	✓

ESSENTIALS	✓	FOR THE JOURNEY	✓

		IMPORTANT DOCUMENTS	✓

CRUISE PACKING CHECKLIST

CLOTHING	✓	ESSENTIALS	✓

CRUISE EXCURSION PLANNER

ACTIVITY / EXCURSION OVERVIEW:

EST COST OF EXCURSION: _____

INCLUSIONS:	✓	**EXCLUSIONS:**	✓
FOOD & DRINK:	☐		☐
TRANSPORTATION:	☐		☐
GRATUITY:	☐		☐

ACTUAL COST: _____

IMPORTANT INFORMATION:

CONTACT: _____   PHONE #: _____

MEET UP TIME: _____   WHAT TO BRING: _____

ADDRESS: _____

CRUISE EXCURSION PLANNER

ACTIVITY / EXCURSION OVERVIEW:

EST COST OF EXCURSION: _____

INCLUSIONS:	✓		**EXCLUSIONS:**	✓
FOOD & DRINK:	☐		_____	☐
TRANSPORTATION:	☐		_____	☐
GRATUITY:	☐		_____	☐

ACTUAL COST: _____

IMPORTANT INFORMATION:

CONTACT: _____ PHONE #: _____

MEET UP TIME: _____ WHAT TO BRING: _____

ADDRESS: _____

CRUISE PORT PLANNER

DESTINATION: DATE:

THINGS TO DO / SEE:

WHERE TO EAT:

TRANSPORTATION DETAILS:

OTHER INFORMATION:

RETURN TO SHIP BY:

CRUISE PORT PLANNER

DESTINATION:	DATE:

THINGS TO DO / SEE:

WHERE TO EAT:

TRANSPORTATION DETAILS:

OTHER INFORMATION:

RETURN TO SHIP BY:

CRUISE PORT PLANNER

DESTINATION: DATE:

THINGS TO DO / SEE:

WHERE TO EAT:

TRANSPORTATION DETAILS:

OTHER INFORMATION:

RETURN TO SHIP BY:

CRUISE PORT PLANNER

DESTINATION:	DATE:

THINGS TO DO / SEE:

WHERE TO EAT:

TRANSPORTATION DETAILS:

OTHER INFORMATION:

RETURN TO SHIP BY:

CRUISE PORT PLANNER

DESTINATION: DATE:

THINGS TO DO / SEE:

WHERE TO EAT:

TRANSPORTATION DETAILS:

OTHER INFORMATION:

RETURN TO SHIP BY:

CRUISE PORT PLANNER

DESTINATION:	DATE:

THINGS TO DO / SEE:

WHERE TO EAT:

TRANSPORTATION DETAILS:

OTHER INFORMATION:

RETURN TO SHIP BY:

CRUISE PORT PLANNER

DESTINATION: DATE:

THINGS TO DO / SEE:

WHERE TO EAT:

TRANSPORTATION DETAILS:

OTHER INFORMATION:

RETURN TO SHIP BY:

CRUISE PORT PLANNER

DESTINATION: DATE:

THINGS TO DO / SEE:

WHERE TO EAT:

TRANSPORTATION DETAILS:

OTHER INFORMATION:

RETURN TO SHIP BY:

CRUISE PORT PLANNER

DESTINATION: DATE:

THINGS TO DO / SEE:

WHERE TO EAT:

TRANSPORTATION DETAILS:

OTHER INFORMATION:

RETURN TO SHIP BY:

CRUISE PORT PLANNER

DESTINATION:	DATE:

THINGS TO DO / SEE:

☐
☐
☐
☐
☐
☐
☐

WHERE TO EAT:

☐
☐
☐
☐
☐
☐
☐

TRANSPORTATION DETAILS:

☐
☐
☐
☐
☐

OTHER INFORMATION:

☐
☐
☐
☐
☐

RETURN TO SHIP BY:

CRUISE PORT PLANNER

DESTINATION: DATE:

THINGS TO DO / SEE:

WHERE TO EAT:

TRANSPORTATION DETAILS:

OTHER INFORMATION:

RETURN TO SHIP BY:

CRUISE PORT PLANNER

DESTINATION: DATE:

THINGS TO DO / SEE:

WHERE TO EAT:

TRANSPORTATION DETAILS:

OTHER INFORMATION:

RETURN TO SHIP BY:

CRUISE PORT PLANNER

DESTINATION: | DATE:

THINGS TO DO / SEE:

☐
☐
☐
☐
☐
☐
☐

WHERE TO EAT:

☐
☐
☐
☐
☐
☐
☐

TRANSPORTATION DETAILS:

☐
☐
☐
☐
☐

OTHER INFORMATION:

☐
☐
☐
☐
☐

RETURN TO SHIP BY:

CRUISE PORT PLANNER

DESTINATION: DATE:

THINGS TO DO / SEE:

- [ ]
- [ ]
- [ ]
- [ ]
- [ ]
- [ ]
- [ ]

WHERE TO EAT:

- [ ]
- [ ]
- [ ]
- [ ]
- [ ]
- [ ]
- [ ]

TRANSPORTATION DETAILS:

- [ ]
- [ ]
- [ ]
- [ ]
- [ ]

OTHER INFORMATION:

- [ ]
- [ ]
- [ ]
- [ ]
- [ ]

RETURN TO SHIP BY:

ALL ABOARD!

PRE-CRUISE TO DO LIST & CHECKLIST

1 MONTH BEFORE

2 WEEKS BEFORE

1 WEEK BEFORE

2 DAYS BEFORE

24 HOURS BEFORE

DAY OF TRAVEL

CRUISE PLANNER

WEEK OF:

MONDAY	TUESDAY	WEDNESDAY	THURSDAY
TO DO	TO DO	TO DO	TO DO
MEALS	MEALS	MEALS	MEALS

FRIDAY	SATURDAY	SUNDAY	NOTES
TO DO	TO DO	TO DO	
MEALS	MEALS	MEALS	MEALS

CRUISE PLANNER

WEEK OF:

MONDAY	TUESDAY	WEDNESDAY	THURSDAY
TO DO	TO DO	TO DO	TO DO
MEALS	MEALS	MEALS	MEALS

FRIDAY	SATURDAY	SUNDAY	NOTES
TO DO	TO DO	TO DO	
MEALS	MEALS	MEALS	MEALS

CRUISING TO DO LIST

CRUISE BUCKET LIST

PLACES I WANT TO VISIT:

THINGS I WANT TO SEE:

TOP 3 DESTINATIONS:

CRUISE ITINERARY

Monday

Tuesday

Wednesday

Thursday

Friday

Saturday

Sunday

CRUISE ITINERARY

Monday

Tuesday

Wednesday

Thursday

Friday

Saturday

Sunday

CRUISE ITINERARY

Monday

Tuesday

Wednesday

Thursday

Friday

Saturday

Sunday

CRUISE OVERVIEW

MONTH:

MONDAY	TUESDAY	WEDNESDAY	THURSDAY	FRIDAY	SATURDAY	SUNDAY

CRUISE ACTIVITIES

WEEKLY ACTIVITY TRACKER:

	M	T	W	T	F	S	S
	○	○	○	○	○	○	○
	○	○	○	○	○	○	○
	○	○	○	○	○	○	○
	○	○	○	○	○	○	○
	○	○	○	○	○	○	○
	○	○	○	○	○	○	○
	○	○	○	○	○	○	○
	○	○	○	○	○	○	○
	○	○	○	○	○	○	○
	○	○	○	○	○	○	○
	○	○	○	○	○	○	○
	○	○	○	○	○	○	○
	○	○	○	○	○	○	○
	○	○	○	○	○	○	○

DAILY ACTIVITY PLANNER

DAILY ITINERARY

ACTIVITY: _____

TIME: _____

LOCATION: _____

WEATHER: ☀ ⛅ 🌦 ☁ ⛈

MEAL PLANNER

DAILY EXPENSES

TOTAL COST: [   ]

TOP ACTIVITIES

TIME: SCHEDULE:

NOTES:

DAILY ACTIVITY PLANNER

DAILY ITINERARY

ACTIVITY: _____

TIME: _____

LOCATION: _____

WEATHER: ☀ ⛅ 🌦 ☁ ⛈

MEAL PLANNER

DAILY EXPENSES

_____ _____

_____ _____

_____ _____

_____ _____

TOTAL COST: [_____]

TOP ACTIVITIES

TIME:	SCHEDULE:

NOTES:

DAILY ACTIVITY PLANNER

DAILY ITINERARY

ACTIVITY: _____

TIME: _____

LOCATION: _____

WEATHER: ☀ ⛅ 🌦 ☁ ⛈

MEAL PLANNER

DAILY EXPENSES

_____   _____

_____   _____

_____   _____

_____   _____

TOTAL COST: [   ]

TOP ACTIVITIES

TIME:	SCHEDULE:

NOTES:

DAILY ACTIVITY PLANNER

DAILY ITINERARY

ACTIVITY: _____

TIME: _____

LOCATION: _____

WEATHER: ☀ ⛅ 🌦 ☁ ⛈

MEAL PLANNER

DAILY EXPENSES

TOTAL COST: [   ]

TOP ACTIVITIES

TIME: SCHEDULE:

NOTES:

DAILY ACTIVITY PLANNER

DAILY ITINERARY

ACTIVITY: _____

TIME: _____

LOCATION: _____

WEATHER: ☀ ⛅ 🌦 ☁ ⛈

MEAL PLANNER

DAILY EXPENSES

TOTAL COST: [_____]

TOP ACTIVITIES

TIME: SCHEDULE:

NOTES:

DAILY ACTIVITY PLANNER

DAILY ITINERARY

ACTIVITY: _____

TIME: _____

LOCATION: _____

WEATHER: ☀ ⛅ 🌦 ☁ ⛈

MEAL PLANNER

TOP ACTIVITIES

TIME:	SCHEDULE:

DAILY EXPENSES

TOTAL COST: [ ]

NOTES:

DAILY ACTIVITY PLANNER

DAILY ITINERARY

ACTIVITY: _____

TIME: _____

LOCATION: _____

WEATHER: ☀ ⛅ 🌦 ☁ ⛈

MEAL PLANNER

DAILY EXPENSES

_____ _____

_____ _____

_____ _____

_____ _____

_____ _____

TOTAL COST: [_____]

TOP ACTIVITIES

TIME:	SCHEDULE:

NOTES:

DAILY ACTIVITY PLANNER

DAILY ITINERARY

ACTIVITY: _____

TIME: _____

LOCATION: _____

WEATHER:

MEAL PLANNER

DAILY EXPENSES

_____ _____

_____ _____

_____ _____

_____ _____

TOTAL COST: [_____]

TOP ACTIVITIES

TIME:	SCHEDULE:

NOTES:

DAILY ACTIVITY PLANNER

DAILY ITINERARY

ACTIVITY: _____

TIME: _____

LOCATION: _____

WEATHER: ☀ ⛅ 🌦 ☁ ⛈

MEAL PLANNER

TOP ACTIVITIES

TIME: SCHEDULE:

DAILY EXPENSES

TOTAL COST: [   ]

NOTES:

DAILY ACTIVITY PLANNER

DAILY ITINERARY

ACTIVITY: _____

TIME: _____

LOCATION: _____

WEATHER:

MEAL PLANNER

DAILY EXPENSES

TOTAL COST: [   ]

TOP ACTIVITIES

TIME:	SCHEDULE:

NOTES:

DAILY ACTIVITY PLANNER

DAILY ITINERARY

ACTIVITY: _____

TIME: _____

LOCATION: _____

WEATHER: ☀ ⛅ 🌦 ☁ ⛈

MEAL PLANNER

DAILY EXPENSES

TOTAL COST: [   ]

TOP ACTIVITIES

TIME:	SCHEDULE:

NOTES:

DAILY ACTIVITY PLANNER

DAILY ITINERARY

ACTIVITY: _____

TIME: _____

LOCATION: _____

WEATHER:

MEAL PLANNER

DAILY EXPENSES

_____

_____   _____

_____   _____

_____   _____

_____   _____

TOTAL COST: [   ]

TOP ACTIVITIES

TIME:	SCHEDULE:

NOTES:

CRUISE FRIENDS

FRIENDS ARE FOREVER

NAME:

PHONE NUMBER:

ADDRESS:

CABIN #:

FRIENDS ARE FOREVER

NAME:

PHONE NUMBER:

ADDRESS:

CABIN #:

FRIENDS ARE FOREVER

NAME:

PHONE NUMBER:

ADDRESS:

CABIN #:

FRIENDS ARE FOREVER

NAME:

PHONE NUMBER:

ADDRESS:

CABIN #:

There's Nothing Like Cruising Life!

CRUISE FRIENDS

FRIENDS ARE FOREVER

NAME:

PHONE NUMBER:

ADDRESS:

CABIN #:

FRIENDS ARE FOREVER

NAME:

PHONE NUMBER:

ADDRESS:

CABIN #:

FRIENDS ARE FOREVER

NAME:

PHONE NUMBER:

ADDRESS:

CABIN #:

FRIENDS ARE FOREVER

NAME:

PHONE NUMBER:

ADDRESS:

CABIN #:

There's Nothing Like Cruising Life!

CRUISE FRIENDS

FRIENDS ARE FOREVER

NAME:

PHONE NUMBER:

ADDRESS:

CABIN #:

FRIENDS ARE FOREVER

NAME:

PHONE NUMBER:

ADDRESS:

CABIN #:

FRIENDS ARE FOREVER

NAME:

PHONE NUMBER:

ADDRESS:

CABIN #:

FRIENDS ARE FOREVER

NAME:

PHONE NUMBER:

ADDRESS:

CABIN #:

There's Nothing Like Cruising Life!

CRUISE FRIENDS

FRIENDS ARE FOREVER

NAME:

PHONE NUMBER:

ADDRESS:

CABIN #:

FRIENDS ARE FOREVER

NAME:

PHONE NUMBER:

ADDRESS:

CABIN #:

FRIENDS ARE FOREVER

NAME:

PHONE NUMBER:

ADDRESS:

CABIN #:

FRIENDS ARE FOREVER

NAME:

PHONE NUMBER:

ADDRESS:

CABIN #:

There's Nothing Like Cruising Life!

MY CRUISE AGENDA

MY CRUISE JOURNAL

DATE:

What I Did Today:

Highlight of the Day:

Thoughts & Reflections:

MY CRUISE JOURNAL

DATE:

What I Did Today:

Highlight of the Day:

Thoughts & Reflections:

MY CRUISE JOURNAL

DATE:

What I Did Today:

Highlight of the Day:

Thoughts & Reflections:

MY CRUISE JOURNAL

DATE:

What I Did Today:

Highlight of the Day:

Thoughts & Reflections:

MY CRUISE JOURNAL

DATE:

What I Did Today:

Highlight of the Day:

Thoughts & Reflections:

MY CRUISE JOURNAL

DATE:

What I Did Today:

Highlight of the Day:

Thoughts & Reflections:

MY CRUISE JOURNAL

DATE:

What I Did Today:

Highlight of the Day:

Thoughts & Reflections:

MY CRUISE JOURNAL

DATE:

What I Did Today:

Highlight of the Day:

Thoughts & Reflections:

MY CRUISE JOURNAL

DATE:

What I Did Today:

Highlight of the Day:

Thoughts & Reflections:

MY CRUISE JOURNAL

DATE:

What I Did Today:

Highlight of the Day:

Thoughts & Reflections:

MY CRUISE JOURNAL

DATE:

What I Did Today:

Highlight of the Day:

Thoughts & Reflections:

MY CRUISE JOURNAL

DATE:

What I Did Today:

Highlight of the Day:

Thoughts & Reflections:

MY CRUISE JOURNAL

DATE:

What I Did Today:

Highlight of the Day:

Thoughts & Reflections:

MY CRUISE JOURNAL

DATE:

What I Did Today:

Highlight of the Day:

Thoughts & Reflections:

Made in United States
Orlando, FL
26 May 2023

33500197R00083